Doormaking For Beginners

Complete Guide To Build And Seal Your Door

Copyright@2023

Cap Grey

Table of content

CHAPTER ONE 3

Instructional Guide To Make A Door ..3

Section 1-Cutting Of The Main Door

Panel 4

Section 2-Embellishing A Blank Door

Panel With Accents 11

Section 3-Completing The Door, And

Mounting It......................................21

CHAPTER TWO 32

Instructional Guide To Seal a Door....32

Section 1-Checking And Cleaning The

Entranceway (Doorway) To The

Building......................................33

Section 2-Taking Measurement Of The

Door..41

Section 3-Installation Of The Weather

Stripping 48

CHAPTER ONE

Instructional Guide To Make A Door

In today's world, you can go to almost any home improvement shop and get a door that has already been cut and is ready to be hung. But what if you want something that is a little bit more sturdy, or what if you need to cover a doorway that is an unusual size? Make a go at building your own door! Getting the necessary measurements is as easy as picking up a piece of plywood measuring 4 feet (1.2 meters) by 8 feet (2.4 meters) and cutting it to those specifications. If you want to give your homemade door a little bit more aesthetic appeal, you may utilize scrap plywood to cut stiles, a centre panel, or other embellishments.

Section 1-Cutting Of The Main Door Panel

1-Take measurements of the doorway through which you will be placing/installing your door.

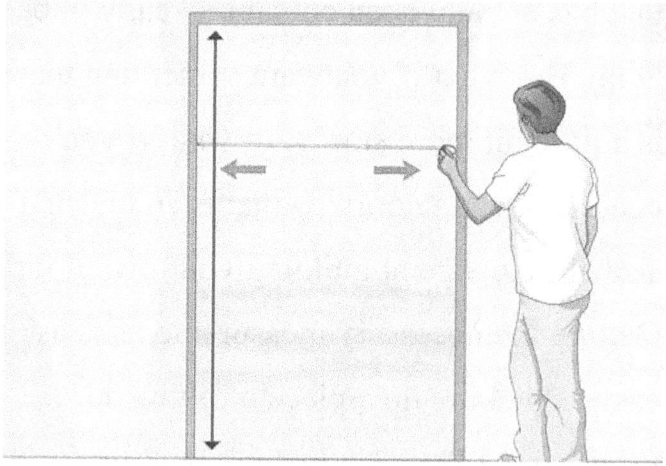

You will first need to determine the precise dimensions of your door before moving on to the gluing and sanding stages of the project. You may determine the height and breadth of your vacant doorway by first dragging a measuring tape down one of the sides, and then extending it over the top.

- Ensure you jot your dimensions down. When you are cutting the panel for your door later on, you are going to need to go back to them for reference.

2-Get a piece of plywood with a thickness of $^1/_2$ inch (1.3 cm), measuring 4 feet (1.2 m) by 8 feet (2.4 m) in size.

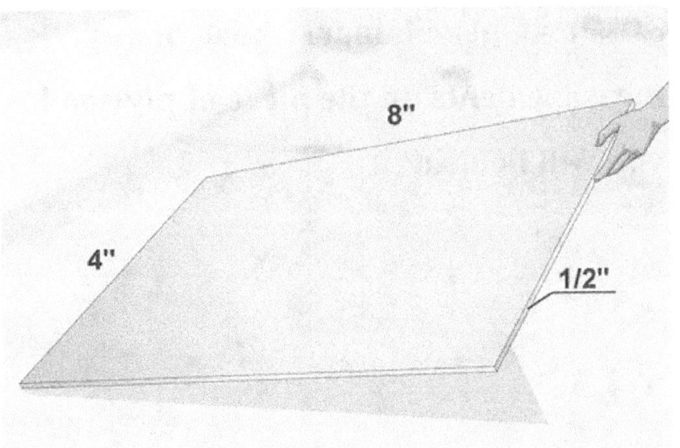

Get on down to the neighborhood home improvement shop or hardware store as soon as you can and pick up a piece of plywood to use as the main panel of your brand-new door. Plywood with a thickness of $^1/_2$ inch (1.3 cm) will work the best for a typical interior door.

- A door made from a single piece of plywood will have a structure that is significantly more robust than the hollow-bodied version that is often used in residential building.

3-Using a pencil, mark the doorway measurements on the piece of plywood you will be using.

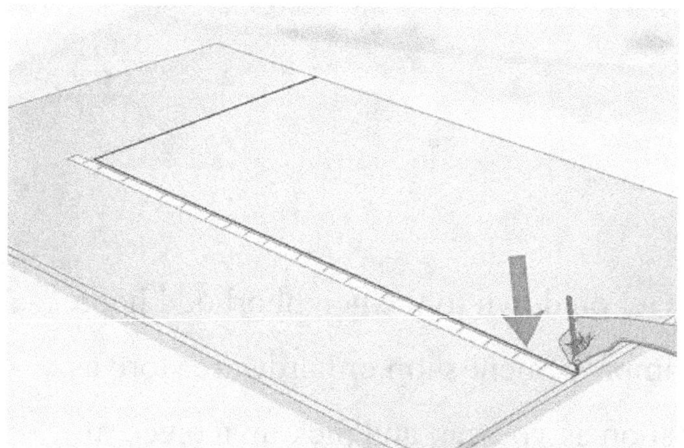

A line should be drawn over the top of the plywood to show the width, and another line should be drawn down the length of the plywood to match to the height of the doorway. This information on the dimensions should have been captured earlier. Your door panel will have a basic outline when this step has been completed.

- To ensure that your lines are exact and straight, you may check them using a ruler or a straight edge. Otherwise, you run the risk of getting a door that doesn't quite close properly!

4-Using a circular saw, cut the plywood to the required proportions so that it may be used.

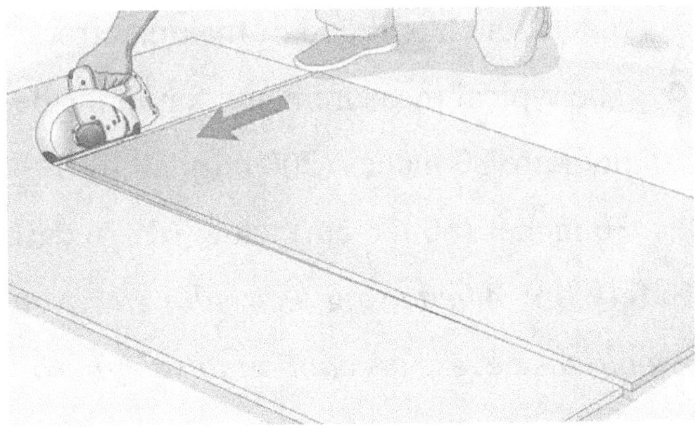

In order to remove the surplus material from the edges of the plywood sheet, gently move the saw blade over the sheet while following the height and breadth lines that you just established. When it is time to make your second cut, dependent on how your work bench is organized, you will need to adjust either the plywood or the saw in order to complete the task successfully.

- By laying a separate piece of timber along your measuring lines, you will be able to make cuts that are cleaner and reduce the likelihood of making errors.
- The typical measurements for an inside door are 80 inches (200 cm) tall by 24–30 inches (60–76 cm) wide (61–76 cm).

Safety tip: *When using a circular saw, you should take every precaution to safeguard* *your hands and eyes by always wearing gloves and goggles.*

5-Sand the whole door panel until it is smooth.

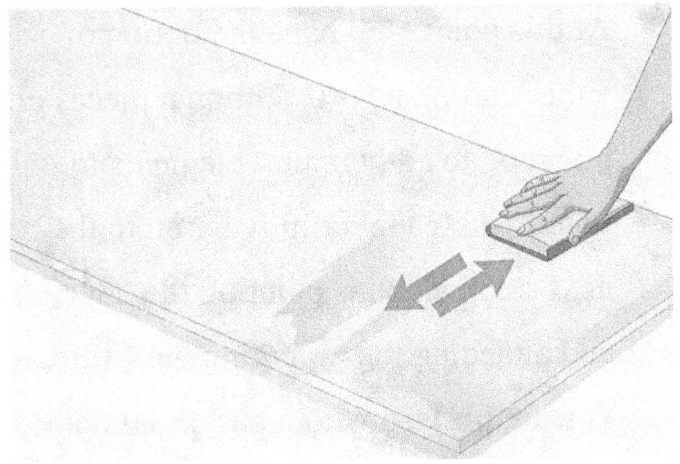

To ensure that the exterior surface is uniform and smooth, sand both sides of the panel using an electric sander or a sheet of high-grit sandpaper. Apply the same amount of pressure throughout the process. After you have finished sanding both sides of the panel, you should move on to the panel's edges.

- To prevent the panel from moving as you sand the edges, you may need to clamp it to another surface or prop it up against anything else.

- At this point, you have the option of either cutting a few additional pieces of plywood to add textural elements to your blank panel or moving on to the next step, which is painting the door and attaching the mounting hardware, if you are pleased with a basic, flat door.

Section 2-Embellishing A Blank Door Panel With Accents

1-Cut the rest plywood into strips that are 10–11 centimeters long and 4–4.5 inches wide.

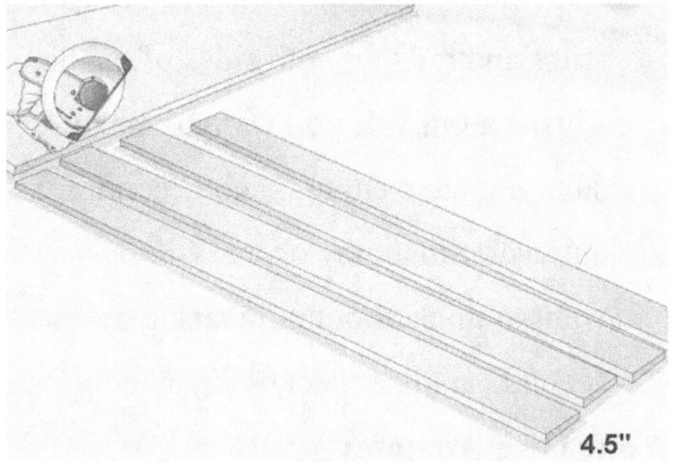

You could want to manufacture a set of straightforward stiles and rails for your door in order to give it some more depth, but this will depend on how much scrap plywood you have left over. If the height of the main door panel is 80 inches (200 cm) and the width is 25 inches (64 cm), you should have sufficient leftover material for about 4 parts measuring 80 inches (200 cm) by 4.5 inches (11 cm) and 6 sections measuring 16 inches (41 cm) by 4.5 inches (11 cm).

- Remember that you will need to install stiles and rails on both sides of the door. This is a must. If you want to make sure you have enough and account for any waste that may occur, you may want to think about purchasing a second, smaller sheet of plywood.

Your Own Anatomy

Stiles are narrow pieces of wood that are put in a vertical orientation to frame the sides of a door. In a similar fashion, rails are installed across the top, bottom, and centre of the door to finish frame it and give it a feeling of symmetry.

2-Apply construction glue to the panel's edges where the stiles will be attached, and then attach the stiles.

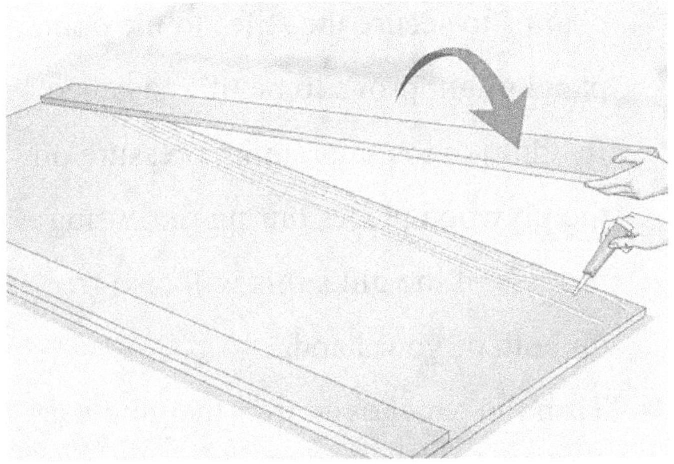

Apply two to three lines of glue down the length of the panel on both of its sides. After that, place a strip that is 80 inches (200 centimeters) long and 4.5 inches (11 centimeters) wide over each side, and then push it down into the adhesive. Maintain constant pressure on the stile pieces for three to five minutes, or until the adhesive has sufficiently hardened to secure them in place, whichever comes first.

- Utilizing a vice or a pair of table clamps to secure the stiles to the door panel might prove to be of assistance. In addition to maintaining pressure on the plywood pieces during the curing process of the glue, this will also free up both of your hands.
- Turn the panel over after the glue has fully cured, and then connect the two remaining stile pieces to the side that is facing the other direction.

3-Cut your remaining plywood strips to a length of 16 inches (41 cm) by sawing them into six portions.

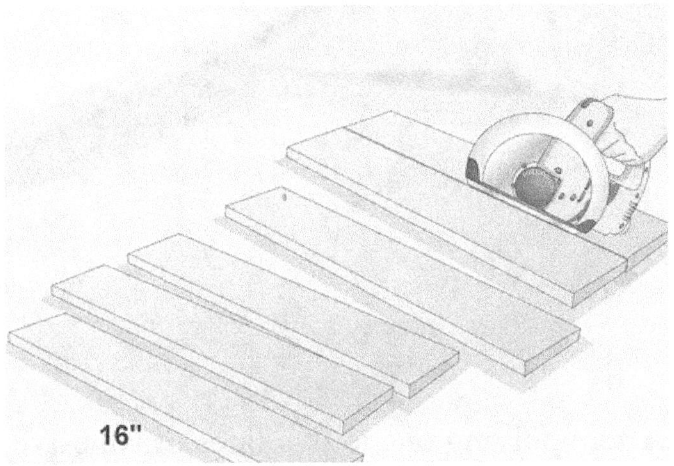

These portions will function as your rails in the structure. After they have been cut, they will easily slide in between the stiles, which should have a distance of precisely 16 inches (41 cm) between them.

● You need to take individual measurements for each of your rails, and then cut them in order to get them all to the same length.

4-Secure the rails to the door panel by gluing them in place.

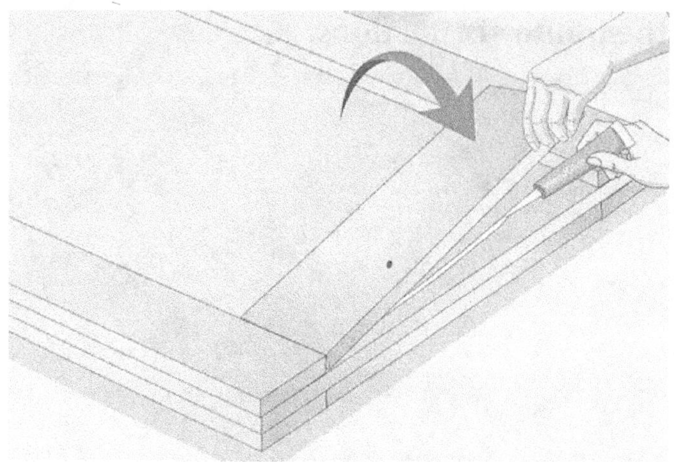

After applying one to two lines of adhesive to the reverse side of each of your rail pieces, place them in the spaces in between stiles at the top, bottom, and centre of the door. Clamp a single rail set at a time before going on to the next rail set in the sequence. It is essential that you do not forget to take into consideration the fact that you will need to perform this action on both sides of the door.

- If you want to be sure that your center rail is in the right place, you should draw a line widthwise across the middle of the panel, or the mark that is located at 40 inches (100 cm), and then use that line as a reference while you are putting it in place and gluing it.
- Makeshift clamps may be created by pressing down on the middle rails with a heavy item that has a level base.

5-Add ornamental trim to give your door additional aesthetic appeal (optional).

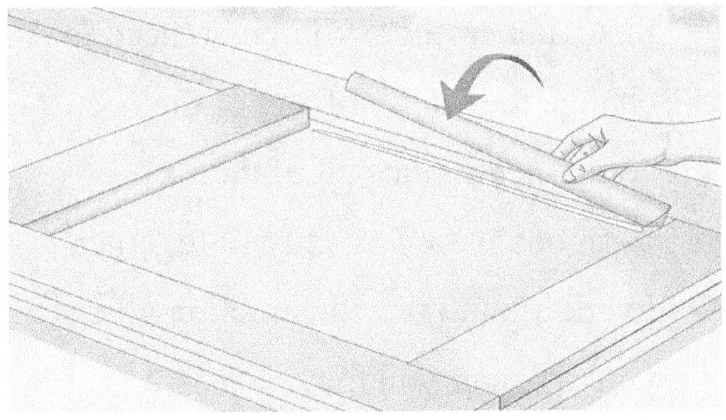

If you want your door to have a more finished appearance, you should buy a few feet of wooden moulding in the style that you desire and then cut it to fit around the inside edges of the panel where even the stiles and rails meet. You'll need a total of 8 pieces measuring 33.25 inches (84.5 centimeters) and 8 parts measuring 16 inches (41 centimeters) (4 for each side of the door). Attach them with glue next to the stiles and rails.

- Using a saw set at a 45-degree angle, cut the ends of each segment of trim. In this manner, there will be no need to change the length of any of the components since all of the components will readily fit together.
- In addition to the construction glue you're using, you may also use finishing nails measuring 1.25 inches

(3.2 centimeters) to offer an extra layer
of protection.

Section 3-Completing The Door, And Mounting It

1-Drill holes for the lockset.

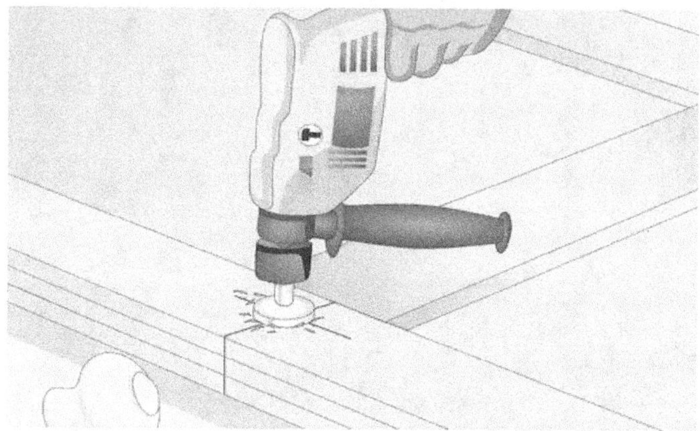

Open up a hole at the end of the door in which the knob or handle would go by using a cordless drill equipped with a hole saw attachment that measures 2.125 inches (5.40 cm) in diameter. After drilling through one side up to its midpoint, turn the door over and continue boring through the other side. After you have completed this step, you will need to switch to a hole saw that is 1 in (2.5 cm) in diameter and drill right into the edge of the door to provide space for the latch.

Optimum Efficiency

If you want the greatest possible results, you should seriously consider purchasing a hole-boring template. Your final job will be neater and more productive if you screw them into place around the edge of the door. This will make the procedure of installing the lockset more easier and straightforward.

2-To improve the look of your door, paint or stain it.

You can now concentrate on giving your door a finish that will make it stand out after you've completed the assembly of it. Make use of a handheld sash brush to apply two to three coats of water-based alkyd paint in the hue of your choosing. In between applications, leave the paint to dry completely. Use a foam brush or cloth to apply stains, and then add or remove the stain in very small increments until you obtain the appropriate level of color saturation.

- The majority of paints that are water-based need around 24 hours to dry fully. If you decide to stain your door instead of painting it, you should wait anywhere from 12 to 24 hours, based on the product you are using, before applying a second layer.

- You should plan on applying at least two coats if you want the finish to be as smooth and consistent as possible.

3-If your door can be opened to the outside, you should choose a sealant that is water-resistant.

It is a good idea to treat your door with a weatherproofing product before installing it in a structure such as a garage, shed, workshop, or any building of a similar kind. Apply a layer of clear polyurethane sealer or wood varnish to each and every surface of the door, including the outside edges, using a paintbrush. You may get the sealant deeper into grooved trim and other curved sections by working the tip of your brush into the region.

- All of your hard work may be undone if your door were to eventually warp, break, or split as a result of prolonged exposure to the weather.

- Even if you want to hang your door on the inside of your home, applying a clear coat will protect its surface from flaking and fading.

- The fumes that are produced by sealants and varnishes are often rather powerful. To optimize the airflow in your workstation, keep surrounding doors and windows unlocked and, if at all feasible, use a window crack.

**4-Attach the latch and the knob or
handle, whatever you like**.

You may secure the latch to the door using
the screws that are supplied by sliding it
into the hole that is 1 in (2.5 cm) in
diameter and located on the internal edge
of the door. After ensuring that the two
sides of the knob or handle are properly
aligned on each side of the 2.125-inch
(5.40-centimeter) hole, secure the faceplate
by tightening the screws all the way around
it.

- If the hardware for your latch doesn't fit flush with the edge of the door, you might have to carve a shallow mortise for it by chiselling away the area around it. This will enable the hardware to lay flush with the edge of the door. Because of this, it will be able to securely seat itself into the wood.

- When installing the latch, be sure to do it in such a way that the rounded edge is towards the door jamb. If you put it in the wrong way around, you won't be able to get the door to shut until you turn the knob or handle in all way.

- Be sure that any door hardware that has a lever on it is installed the correct way around before you proceed.

5-Attach the door's hinges and then tighten them.

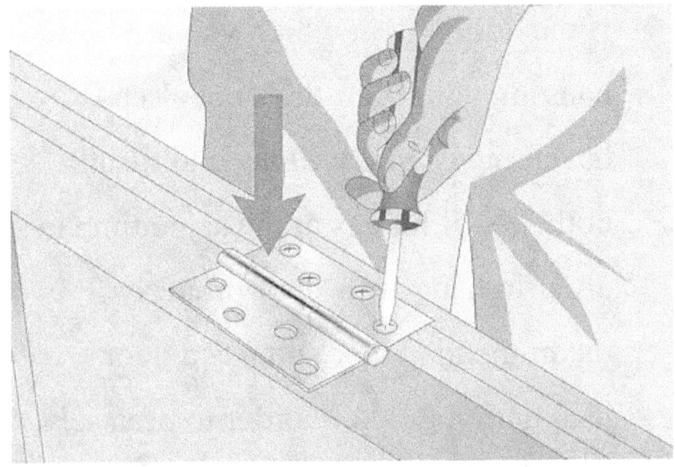

Utilize a measuring tape to determine the distance that exists between the hinges that are already installed on your doorframe. Put the new hinges on the door's edge that faces the inside of the room, and then use a pencil to draw a circle around them. Then, using a hammer and chisel, cut out a shallow mortise in each spot where the hinges will be attached. At last, position the hinges so that they fit into the depressions, and then use a cordless drill to secure them in place.

- If the doorway in which you are hanging your door does not already have hinges, you will need to install both sets of hinges at the same time in order to hang your door properly. It is recommended that you use a door installation guide in order to precisely locate where your door frame hinges should be placed and how far apart they need to be spaced.

6-Attach your door to its frame by inserting its hinges into the corresponding holes in the door frame.

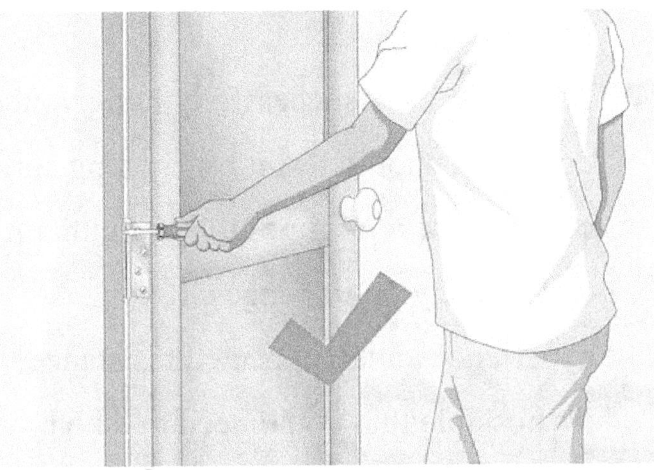

The only thing left to do at this point is to hang your finished door. Raise the door to a height that allows the two sets of hinges to interlock, then slip the hinge pins into the hole at the top of each hinge and hammer them firmly into place. You're done!

- While you are putting the hinges on the door, you may make makeshift shims out of scraps of wood or pieces of cardboard that have been folded in order to keep the door at the right height.

- After you have successfully hung your door, you should test it by opening and closing it several times to ensure that it slides freely on its hinges. If you experience any unexpected resistance, it's possible that you'll need to take it down and give it another go.

CHAPTER TWO

Instructional Guide To Seal a Door

Your house may have drafts because there are spaces surrounding your door that enable air to move through. This will result in a decrease in the effectiveness of both your heating and cooling systems, as well as a potential decrease in the comfort level of your house. On the other hand, sealing a door takes very little time and effort. Determine the locations of any air leaks in your home and seal them using weather stripping to complete the task. After you have applied the weather stripping to your door, the last thing you need to do before reaping the advantages of your freshly sealed door is to check that the door can still be opened and closed without difficulty.

Section 1-Checking And Cleaning The Entranceway (Doorway) To The Building

1-Make sure that your door's hinges are properly tightened.

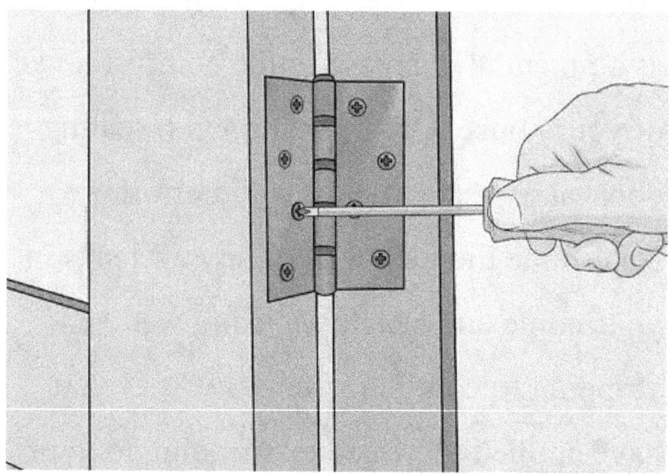

Raise the door using the doorknob as leverage. If you are able to move it upwards, then the hinges are probably not tight enough. Employing a screwdriver, one may further secure the hinges by turning the screws that hold them in place.

- The door moving because of loose hinges is the root cause of some of the drafts. Because of this, you should spend a few minutes to ensure that all of the hardware is adequately tightened before you seal the sides of your door.

- It is a sign that the wood in the hole has been stripped out if the screws that hold the hinge in place spin but will not tighten. In order for the screws to be able to penetrate wood that has not been damaged, you will have to replace them with screws that are either broader or longer. If there is a significant amount of damage to the wood, it is possible that you will need to use wood plugs to replace the holes

and then re-drive new screws into the
plugs.

**2-Determine the current condition of the
aging weather stripping.**

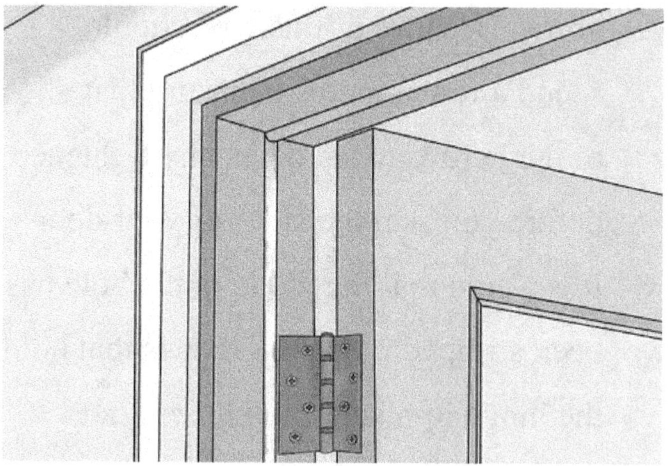

It is possible that the weather stripping that
was previously put on your door has been
distorted or damaged. Check it by moving
your hand around the edge of the door
when it is closed and ensuring that it does
not move. Examine the space between both
the door and the frame to see if air is
passing through it. Put a light mark with a

pencil or a piece of painter's tape in the spots where you can feel air coming in.

● If you are able to detect a draft in locations in which weather stripping installed, you will need to take away the existing weather stripping and install a new seal in its place.

3-Remove any debris from the regions that will later be sealed.

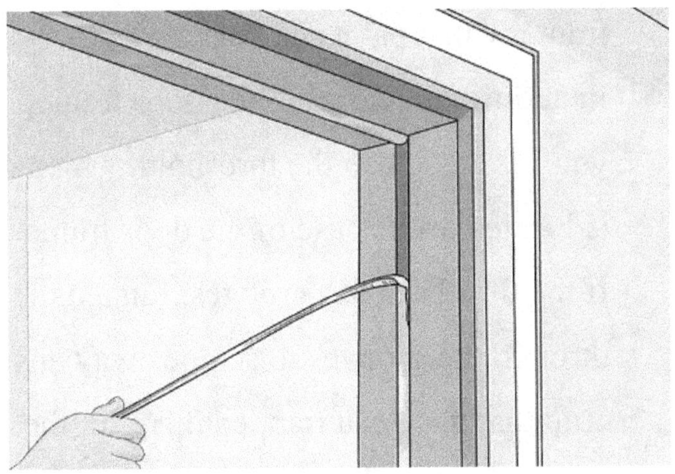

Peel or slide the old weather stripping away from the window and dispose of it if it is damaged or no longer functional. After that, use a wet towel and wash down the door frame as well as the edges of the door itself to remove any apparent dirt and debris that may be present. This will assist you in securing the new weather stripping that you are attaching.

- To remove any debris that has been adhered to the door, door frame, and surrounding areas, scrape the door and frame with a paint scraper.

- In addition to cleaning the door frame, you have to clean the threshold, which is located at the base of the door frame. If the threshold has grooves, run a nail through the grooves to scrape away any crud that has been trapped there. In the event that the threshold has grooves, you should hammer a nail through each groove. Then, to verify that the surfaces are clean, run a cloth that has been

dampened just slightly along the
threshold and the door frame.

4-Go to a shop that specializes in home improvements or hardware and get some brand new weather stripping.

You may choose to install any one of the many various kinds of weather stripping that are on the market today; however, you will need to determine which kind you want to use. Wrapped foam weather stripping is a long-lasting option that works well with gaps of varying sizes and may be applied to the top and sides of your door.

When compared to metal weather stripping, weather stripping with a wooden shell is not only more durable but also simpler to deal with. As a result, this kind of weather stripping is an excellent option for someone who has never sealed doors before. Consider selecting a metal door sweep that has a flexible vinyl flap for the door sweep if you are looking for something that will last longer.

- Installing a metal door sweep that has a flexible vinyl flap is also rather simple, as the metal piece can simply be screwed into place, and then the vinyl flap can be fitted into the metal piece. Storm seals and roller door seals, like brush or auto-lift vinyl seals on roller door bottoms, are among the more advanced options available.

- Be aware that the majority of weather stripping kits only contain weatherstripping for the sides as well as top of your door if you choose to purchase one of these kits. A door sweep is a separate item that must be purchased by you.

- If the carpet is at the same level as or higher than the threshold, rigid door sweeps will not function properly. When using stiff door sweeps is not an option, flexible vinyl bulb weather stripping should be used instead. This fastens to the floor just below the door and connects to the threshold.

- If it is at all feasible, get weatherstripping in a few different thicknesses and test them out on the door to ensure that it will shut properly.

When the incorrect size is used, the
door will simply spring back into place.

Section 2-Taking Measurement Of The Door

1-Take measurements of the top as well as the sides of the door frame.

After closing the door, use a tape measure to take measurements along the top of the door frame. A tape measure should be used to take measurements along both sides of the door frame while the door is still closed.

- It is important to keep in mind that the measurements you take for the top side of the door will have to be taken along the door frame rather than the door itself.

- In order to create an airtight seal, you will need to take measurements and cut pieces of weather stripping so that they are a perfect match on each side. This means that you will need to know the exact length of each side in order to properly cut the weather stripping pieces.

Tip: *A helpful hint is that you should measure each side independently. In most cases, the length of both sides will be the same; nevertheless, mistakes in construction are very prevalent, and as a result, there may be some little differences in length.*

2-Take a measurement at the bottom of the door.

First, open the door, and then use a tape measure to determine the length of the bottom of the door. You will need to take measures for the bottom seal in a different way than you did for the top and side seals. Instead, you will need to take measurements of the bottom of the door itself.

- When you are taking this measurement, you need to be sure that you are facing the inside of the door. This will be the surface that the weather stripping is applied to in the next step.

3-Make a mark corresponding to those dimensions on the weather stripping.

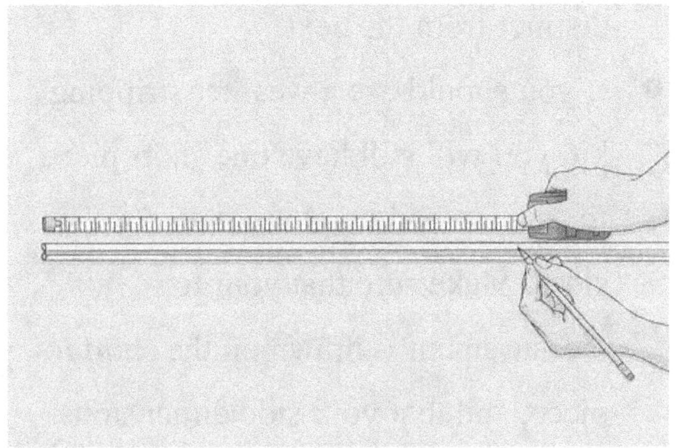

You will need to take precise measurements using a tape measure in order to cut the weather stripping for the top sides of the door that you ordered. Upon the door sweep weather stripping that you purchased, make a mark that corresponds to the length of the bottom of the door.

- Make a mark at each of the lengths using a marker or a sharp pencil. Check that every line you draw is distinct and distinct from the next.

- If you should use a weather stripping kit, you will still have one short piece for the top and two long ones for the sides. Make sure that your top measurement is drawn on the shorter piece, and that your side dimensions are drawn on the longer piece.

4-Cut the weather stripping to the desired length and width.

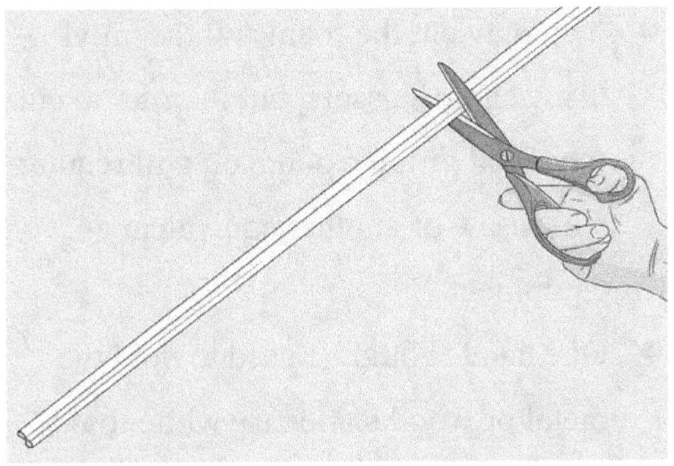

At the points that you just measured out, cut the weather stripping to length. Make sure that your cuts are as even and clean as you can get them in order to have a good seal. In addition to this, you will need to ensure that the ends of the top piece are angled, and that one end of each side piece is angled as well, so that the side pieces can be inserted into the top piece of weather stripping. The bottom ends of your side pieces do not need an angle to be cut into them.

- You may cut the foam and the vinyl using sharp scissors, but in order to cut the metal or the wood, you will require a hacksaw or another equivalent equipment.

- One hand should be used to hold the metal or wood stationary while the other should be used to saw through it. The slower you go, the more likely it is that the cut will be straight.

Section 3-Installation Of The Weather Stripping

1-Secure the uppermost section of the weather stripping using tacks.

After stepping inside, shutting the door, and positioning yourself within, place the weather stripping top piece along the top of your door frame. Nail it into place in a sloppy manner. Hammer in the nails just far enough to ensure that the weather stripping will remain in place.

- It is imperative that you do not complete driving the nails until after you have added the side pieces.

- It is essential that this seal be attached to the door frame and not directly to the door itself.

- Use nails that are 1.25 inches (3.75 cm) in length. To stop the wood from cracking, drive the nails in from each side about two inches (five centimeters) in. In addition, the distance between each nails should be 12 inches (30.5 cm).

Tip: *A helpful hint to keep in mind while installing the weather stripping is that the foam should entirely fill up the space at the top of the frame. On the other hand, it should only compress gently and not too firmly at all. It's possible that the door won't lock if you apply too much pressure.*

2-Tack your side pieces into position.

Put the weather stripping pieces on the sides of your door frame so that they are flush against the frame. It is necessary for your side pieces to be compatible with the door frame rather than the actual door, and the foam should fill in the space surrounding the door. This is done in the same way as the top piece. Put each side piece where it should be along the side of the door frame, and then use a hammer and nails to secure it in place.

- You will need to file the top angle down if it does not allow the top piece of weather stripping to fit into it. To get the desired degree of precision at these top angles, you might utilize a metal file, sandpaper, or a sanding belt.

- Continue to make minute modifications and double verify your work until you have achieved the desired angle.

- To install the bottom piece of weather stripping in the same manner as the top piece, use nails measuring 1-1/2 inches and position them 2 inches (5 cm) from each end. Each nail should have a distance of 12 inches (30.5 cm) between it and the next nail.

3-Put the seal to the test.

Repeatedly opening and closing the door
will ensure that the weather stripping forms
a good seal when the door is closed. In
order to verify that the weather stripping is
performing as expected, feel the regions
that you identified as having air flow.
When the door is closed, the weather
stripping must form a perfect seal against
the door, and the door itself must be able to
latch and lock securely.

- Take off your weather stripping and
  make any necessary adjustments to its

position in order to obtain a suitable
seal.

**4-Drive the nails into the wood in order
to secure the weather stripping.**

When you are certain that the weather
stripping around the top and sides of the
door is well sealed, you may finish
hammering in the nails. After you have
finished driving the nails in, you should
check the seal one more time. You should
try opening and closing the door to see
whether the seal is still intact.

5-Figure out where on the door the door sweep should be installed in the correct manner.

Put the door sweep along the bottom border of the inside door, but do not yet nail or screw it into position. The bendable part of the door sweep has to come into contact with the highest point of the threshold, but it shouldn't press too hard on it.

● Door sweeps made of metal will often already have screw holes on them.

Make a note on your door using only a pencil or marker indicating where these holes should be placed. First, make a temporary removal of the door sweep, and then drill pilot holes into the parts that have been designated.

- It is important to keep in mind, however, that vinyl door sweeps are mounted on the threshold rather than the door itself. Adjust the strip such that one of its ends is aligned with one of the threshold's ends. Put some pressure on the flanges, which comprise the edges of the strip, and push them firmly into the grooves of the threshold using your hands.

6-Affix the door sweep to the frame.

Make sure that the door sweep is pressed
up against the door's threshold at the
bottom. Put the screws into the pilot holes
that you bored earlier in the process. Make
the sweep secure by screwing it into place
with a screwdriver.

● Put a wooden tapping block on top of
   the weather stripping if you are going
   to be using a vinyl door sweep.
   Applying force with your hammer to
   the block will allow you to push the

flanges of the weatherstripping further into the grooves of the threshold.

6-Perform another test of the seal.

Check the bottom seal by opening and closing the door a few times to see whether it works. The process is finished after the weatherstripping on the sides, top, and bottom has been correctly put in the appropriate locations. Your door ought to be completely sealed at this point.